The Stock Market Flea™

Lessons from the Front

James J Houts

This book is intended for entertainment and historical purposes only. No stock market advice, stock recommendations, or broker/dealer recommendations are intended or implied. The strategies detailed are the author's and may not be suitable for anyone else. Each investor should speak with a professional investment consultant before investing. All the author's reminiscences are from his life, but the characters are fictional, any resemblance to actual people, living or dead is purely coincidental. Images not created by the author were provided by dreamstime Images.

Cheyenne Spring Publishing
1740H Del Range Blvd., Suite 130
Cheyenne, Wyoming 82009
USA

Library of Congress Cataloging-in-Publication Data

Houts, James J.
The Stock Market Flea™: Lessons from the Front / James J. Houts

ISBN 13 978-0615893976
ISBN 10 061589397X

Mei Ling

yinwèi nǐ jiào wǒ nàixin de, píng jing de, hé pǔtōnghuà.

(for teaching me patience, peace and Mandarin.)

The
Stock Market Flea™

Lessons from the Front

James J Houts

There is a tide in the affairs of men.
Which, taken at the flood, leads on to fortune;
Omitted, all the voyage of their life
is bound in shallows and in miseries.
On such a full sea are we now afloat,
And we must take the current when it serves,
Or lose our ventures.

—William Shakespeare

Overture

Introduction

Lessons from the front

In the gritty 1961 movie, *The Hustler*, Paul Newman plays "Fast Eddie" Felson, as young small-time pool shark on his way to the big time. Directed and produced by Robert Rossen, the movie also stars Jackie Gleason as Minnesota Fats, George C. Scott as Bert and Piper Laurie as Sarah. In a dirty, small-town bar Eddie hustles the local pool hero, but his pride overwhelms his common sense and he uses all of his huge talent to humiliate the local player and enrage the bar's murderous clientele. After taking a beating in the filthy bathroom Eddie makes his way back to his dingy hotel room and Sarah. When a shocked Sarah asks him what's happened, Eddie moans, "I got beat up. They...broke my thumbs... Oh, they broke my thumbs."

***

During the late 1990s my job as a sales engineer required I travel most of the time. I was an American expatriate with my primary residence in Manila, Republic of Philippines, my immediate supervisor lived in Houston, Texas, and our corporate headquarters was in Philadelphia, Pennsylvania. I had customers and prospects all over the world and called on them in their home countries. Socializing with other expatriates, whose favorite topics of conversation were the richness of their expat packages and their prowess as world travelers, could be tedious or entertaining – depending on the story and the teller. My favorite boast was that I had negotiated engineering contracts on every continent but Antarctica, and if I discovered there was potential business there, I would certainly book a trip.

Almost every quarter I would purchase a round-the-world flight – as long as you didn't backtrack, you could stop as often as you liked and take as much time as you could stand. I often booked week-end stops in exotic locales.

Eventually my travels took me to Budapest, Hungary. My hotel, located in an ancient, but recently hip section of the city, had a beautiful view of the Danube. After settling into my room, I went out for a walk on Vaci Utca, a street famous for window shopping and cafes, eager to experience a new city and its night life. I was a confident traveler, having braved cities that made the "wild west" of Eastern Europe seem almost bland.

The contents of the many shops were as interesting as the people strolling beside me. Soon, a pretty young woman drew near; evidently captivated by some item beyond a window, she stood very close to me. Finally, she spoke, the first words I had understood on the cobblestoned street. With little opportunity to practice her English skills, a conversation with me would be a great favor. My lucky day. We walked together for a while and as we passed a small open air café, I asked her to join me for a cup of coffee. She readily agreed, but suggested that we cross the street to another café, one that was much "better." Who was I to disagree?

By the time we entered the darkened bistro my new acquaintance had decided to have a drink instead of coffee and this was my preference as well. Then a serendipitous meeting with an old girlfriend was a joyous occasion for my companion, with hugs and kisses all around. The long lost, but newly reunited friend accepted my invitation to join us for a drink. I had a scotch and the girls had sweet looking juice drinks with lots of fruit and ornaments hanging from the rims of the glasses. The ladies must have been *very* thirsty because they downed their drinks and asked for another before I had touched mine. This should have set off my internal alarm, but I was an experienced world traveler, an expatriate, a citizen of the world, and my arrogance overwhelmed my common sense. When they downed their second drinks just as quickly and requested a third, all my bells and whistles went off.

Sure enough, their drinks were a hundred bucks a piece. When I balked at the bill, two burly Russian guys showed up with menacing frowns. So much for the money I had budgeted for week-end play in a new city. These guys had cleaned me out in ten minutes – and since I didn't want my thumbs, or anything else, broken, I paid up. My pride about being a world traveler didn't pass the Budapest test.

Arrogance is one of many emotions that will cause you to lose money in the options market, and avoiding losses is the goal of the Stock Market Flea. Emotion, as explained in the first two books of this series, is the enemy of the options trader.

The many lessons included in this book summarize some of what I learned as I traded stocks and options during the Crash of 2008 and the five years of recovery since. Most of these warnings and rules were spawned from my painful losses, and big wins, during this historic period; though some come from a lifetime of trading and others just from life. But even I wouldn't have the hubris to consider these short statements a basis for an investment plan, or that they are true in every case. After all, trading like a flea helped me avoid the Crash of 2008, but it also kept me from going all-in during the recovery that began in March 2009.

Most of the lessons that follow were included in previously published books of my Stock Market Flea series: *Reminiscences of a Stock Market Flea* and *The Stock Market Flea: Trading the Crash of 2008*. I hope the reader finds them interesting, helpful, and entertaining.

Take your own risks.
Don't share them with others.

If you trade you must start with a plan. That's the easy part. The hard part is you must execute the plan.

When your plan gets trumped by the facts—change the plan.

Selling covered calls. If you have
made profit on a stock and you
don't want to sell it, but you do
want to protect the profits, you can
sell some call options against it.
Your downside protection will be
equal to the price of the call you
sell or in market lingo, write.

If you are lucky enough to get a double, you MUST sell half.

You can't lose if you're playing with the houses money.

When a stock moves up suddenly on news, the temptation is to buy call options to take part in the move,

but the smart play is to buy put options—the stock will usually pull back near to where it traded before the news was released.

A stockbroker is a great guy, but he is a salesman, not an investment expert. You can't depend on him for investment advice.
You are on your own.

VIX is low, time to go.

VIX is high, time to buy.

Don't be slow, Don't be greedy.

Past trades will affect future trading. A big loss could cause you to miss a great opportunity, while a big win could deaden your appreciation of risk.

You need to be able to take a 25 percent loss happily. After all, the market has spoken, telling you that this time, on this trade, you have gotten it wrong. Think of it as saving 75 percent, not as losing 25 percent. Most of the time this will be true.

Do the basics and don't take chances. We don't need to run up the score to win.

Remember: the options market is a zero sum game, for every winner there is a loser.

It's your job to make the other guy lose his money.

Options with less than thirty days left before expiration should not be bought to hold more than a few days. Make it fast or take your lumps.

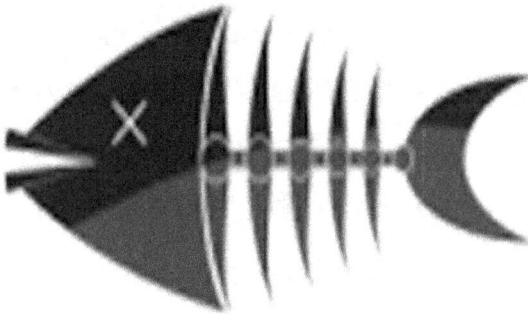

Options held more than three days start to smell like three-day old fish or houseguests.

If you want to own the stock anyway, let in-the-money calls expire. Otherwise don't wait, take the profits before the last few days of the contract and the noise that surrounds the expiration.

When trading options, a flea needs to fight the battle like the North Vietnamese—in close to avoid the artillery. "Grab them by the belt buckle and hang on." In the options market this means buying fewer options nearer the trading price of the underlying security, rather than more options further out.

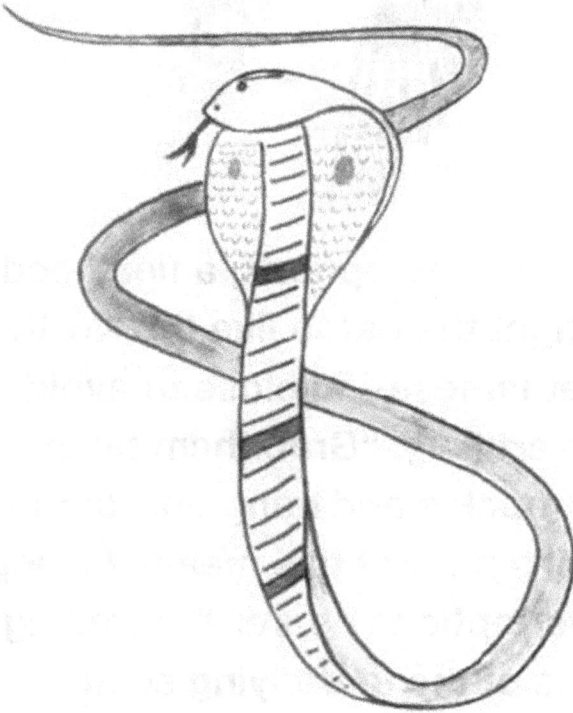

Don't mark duds, or trade options, if mentally or emotionally compromised.

Options spreads are options light—everything about them is slower and lower; the speed, the change, the cost, and the profit.

When you need protection, lay it on. Don't try to get the last few cents in pricing.

Or using the age-old saying, "Don't be penny wise and pound foolish."

Never argue with someone you love about money or investing.

When the CME increases the margin requirements on gold futures, listen to the bell ringing in the top of the market.

The long-term uptrend may hold, but don't fight city hall—get out and watch from the sidelines.

Never buy real estate with cash if you can borrow the money.

There are a lot of reasons I think this. The biggest reason is leverage.

If you can see water from a property (ocean, lake, river, harbor), you can't lose. There is only so much property with water views and people will pay a premium for it. Even if the market turns down, it will come back to you eventually.

In the aquatic world of Venture Capital investing, the sea quickly grows murky and deep. These unhealthy waters create a dangerous environment for conservative investors or retirement savers. There are dozens of risky investments that are more likely to make a profit, and very few that can wipe you out as fast.

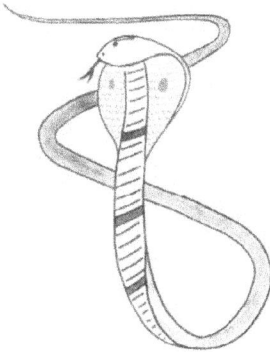

**When it comes to politics, some
things never change, or if they do,
they just get worse.**

Listen to the market. It will tell you all the insider information you will ever need.

If you are willing to take on the risk of owning contracts over the weekend, you should buy them near the close on Friday for the best entry point.

Start every day with a strategy.

When you need to sell options, sell them, don't be a pig. Don't try to get that last inch of profit, you may find you take a huge loss, instead of a smaller-than-desired win.

When buying you can get cute, because the worst that can happen is you don't get the ones you want. There is always another trade.

You can't out-trade the big dog computers. Your only hope is in your strategy, your plan, and your execution.

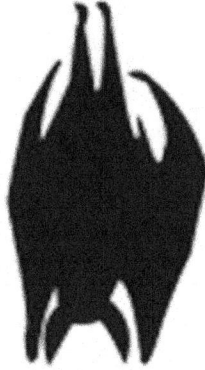

When a stock turns against
your premise and moves hard
opposite your position, you need
to sell as soon as you recognize
it. Yes, it could turn and you could
permanently book the loss, but it
might keep going and you can lose
it all.

The Miracle. You make your plan, do your homework, shop the market, and take your position. Then before you know it everything goes wrong and you find yourself in a huge losing position. Your plan was wrong, and after reevaluating the position you realize that you need a miracle to get out. Then it happens—the angel arrives and the plan starts to work. You either get a small win or you recover to your acceptable loss point. This is the Miracle. Take it. Don't be greedy. Tomorrow is another day.

It is very difficult to call a turn.
Don't try for the last penny of
profit. Jessie Livermore advised,
"Never try to sell at the top."

Livermore recommended, "The
big money is made sitting, not
thinking. Men who can both be
right and sit tight are uncommon."

Buy a house – get homeowner's insurance

Buy a car – get auto insurance

Buy a stock – get option protection

If you absolutely need to hold
onto a call position in spite of the
warnings, you need to buy some
puts as a hedge.
This is called a straddle. This locks
in profits (not the greedy max
profits) and provides protection.

If you have multiple, opposite positions, such as a straddle, the emotions of hope and fear are taken out of the trade and your decision making process is clear of emotion.

If you are smart enough to get a double, you MUST sell at least half.

I don't want to own options near their expiration day; the spice comes out too fast. This is true of the current month and the next.

The flea can't afford to get every bit of profit. When the big dogs move out of a position, the flea gets left behind. Take reasonable profits and don't worry about the money left on the table.

It is better to buy fewer, but more expensive, options with strikes close to the trading price, than to buy more, less expensive, options further from the current price.

It's **OK** to howl at the moon, though it does little good. But you must guard against trading on politics, prejudice or preconception.

It is relatively easy to spot a
bubble, but it is deathly difficult to
know when it will burst.

The most critical part of trading,
and sometimes the most satisfying,
is done while working out of a
losing position.

**Never accept what the so called
"Experts" say as the truth.**

Sometimes what is said is not what is meant. It is up to us to glean the true meaning.

Typically, the price of a good stock increases as the earnings announcement nears ("Buy the rumor"), but will tend to drop off after the announcement is made ("Sell the news").

Owning "stale" options will cause you to miss great new option opportunities. So it is not just the losses or small gains you get out of a poor position, it is the missed opportunity, the opportunity cost of being too distracted to take on a new position.

When the time to sell comes, things will be hectic. Stay calm and check your list for the things you want to sell.

When the market tanks, dig out your buy list.

You can't sell a stock while you have calls sold against it. You need to buy back the calls first.

When your stock is heading south, this is easy to forget.

When you no longer want a very short-term, unprotected stock position, and you decide to lay on option protection, consider buying puts instead of selling calls.

Be very careful and exact when preparing a wish list. When the opportunity comes to use it, you won't have time to check it.

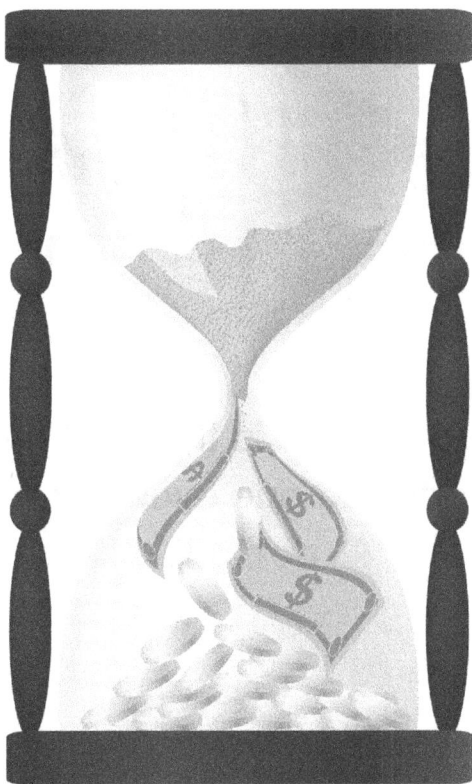

It always feels good to sell. Do it more often.

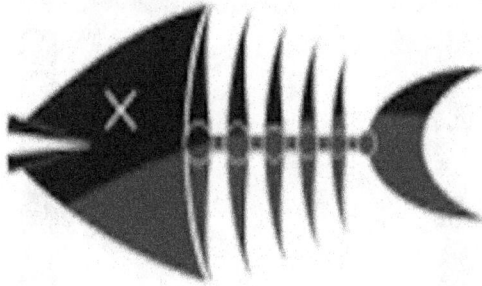

Taking a profit is the best part of the trade. No one ever lost money doing it.

Sell, sell, sell. Early and often.
Bad positions can psychologically
prevent you from reversing course
to take advantage of the trend.

When selecting pricing for limit orders that you want to work when you are not around, don't get greedy. You won't be there to change the order if necessary.

When you have a winner and you hit your target, sell slowly, because the momentum is in your favor. When you have a loser, sell quickly and completely—the trend is going against you.

Don't do anything before 10:00 a.m. The computers are busy balancing out the night's Asia trades at the open. You may get lucky for a big win, but more than likely the markets will change on you at ten. There is no true trend and the big dogs are in the way.

Apple goes into hibernation during the summer. You can play Apple calls in the summer, but the strike dates need to be after October.

Beware the close. At the close you are up against the big dogs and their computers. You can't predict what will happen.

Sell immediately on acts of God, accounting irregularities, executive scandals, SEC investigations, or indictments.

Hope is the very worst strategy for investing or trading.

Emotions and stress can make
you give up. I've sold good option
positions simply because I was
tired – tired of owning a losing
position. And sure enough, as soon
as I sold they moved back up.

Sick stocks stay sick, so don't get in—no matter how cheap they look. Good stocks can get sick— sell right away. Don't over think it. The markets are very superficial.

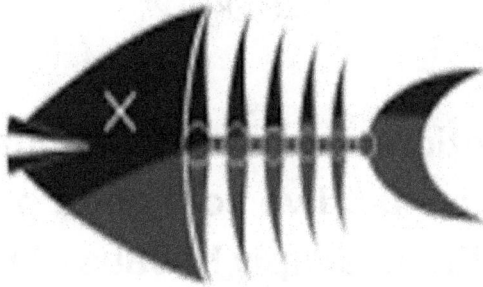

With options you risk less for larger
returns. But you will have more
losers to go with your winners.

Don't ignore narrow Bollinger Bands. Something is going to happen and it usually isn't good.

Don't ignore the "sell half on a double" rule. Don't be slow; Don't be greedy.

No trade stands alone. Your memory of past wins and losses will affect your trading and past emotions will color your view of the present.

Create a plan before you start your trade—where to buy, how much profit needed from the trade (where to sell), where to set your stop-loss points, how much loss can you take (again, where to sell).

But most important, EXECUTE YOUR PLAN.

Options are a diminishing asset; the clock is always running.

Sometimes the miracle moment never shows up.

Don't chase the price. If the computers try to front-run you, stay calm and hold your place. They will come back to you.

There are natural resistance/ support barriers at whole integers (1), each decade (10), and each century (100). These are emotional levels that have nothing to do with the price of the stock or the trend.

Jesse Livermore called this effect "passing par" and said that once a stock breaks through what I call a century, the stock takes off ballistically.

Listen to the market, it will tell you all the insider information, if you will just listen.

Sometimes the market is speaking, but it seems to be speaking in a different language. It always seems obvious later, but at the time, it is babble.

Don't let hope, or the fear of missing a recovery, keep you in a loser. You do confirm and book the losses, but you stop losing.

Sell a loser early if you can and
take the losses. But don't sell when
in a state of panic.

The flea always remembers that it makes you feel good to sell. Win or lose, selling is a pleasant thing, it removes pressure and kills panic. Sell when you can.

Don't play the woulda-coulda-
shoulda Monday-morning-
quarterback game. It won't bring
the trade back and it will make
you crazy. This doesn't mean you
shouldn't learn from your mistakes.

Know your emotional state. Know
that if you are depressed or ill or
otherwise feeling low, you will tend
to not buy into new positions and
you will tend to sell out of winners
too soon. On the other hand, if you
are feeling great, maybe because
you have had a recent win, you
will tend to pay too much for new
positions and you will tend to hold
on to them too long.

When you are trading, trade. Don't be distracted by anything else.

No artificial targets to reach a personal record, to cover a prior loss, or pay for something you want to buy.

When a stock makes a big move up, the options on the winning side of the trade, the calls, will trade actively and there will be good price discovery. But the options on the losing side of the move, the puts—especially puts that have strikes far from where the stock is trading, may not have price discovery until the move is finished.

When a stock like Apple takes off vertically, the call options fill with speculative spice. Always sell your calls at the first break in the vertical trajectory of the stock. Sell them at the first sign of faltering. The spice will protect you, at first.

Your ego is your enemy. When ego gets involved, logic goes out the window.

A trader makes trades, but the trades also make the trader.

You must be smart enough to create a plan, but you must be disciplined enough to work the plan, adjusting to fit the changing marketplace.

Follow the plan. Don't let outside influences change your plan. You can always close out per your plan, reevaluate, and start a new plan. (A new operation, as Livermore would term it.)

When you need to sell a loser, tell yourself, "I'm right on this trade, but it's taking too long. I can do better, faster with my new idea." This avoids the emotional roadblock of admitting you are wrong.

Politics is a wild card. You can't fight city hall and you can't fight the Fed, but you also need to beware of leaders of state, representative assemblies, our congress, mobs in the streets and any other political entity that wields power. Know that they can, and assume they will, surprise and frustrate your plan.

Beware of the EX-Dividend date for covered call positions that are deeply in the money. They will call away your stock to get at the dividend.

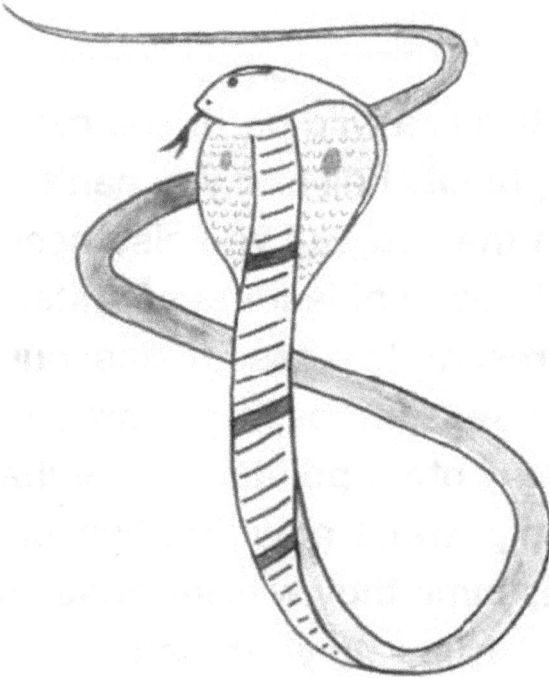

Always keep a trading log. Record every trade; but more important, record why you chose the position you have taken.

If the market moves against you and your premise proves incorrect, the written record of your reasoning makes it easier to justify changing your mind on the trade.

Calculate your ratio of longs to shorts everyday and keep this ratio in front of you while trading. Adjust the ratio to match your confidence in the market. If you are feeling bullish, more long positions; not so confident, more short positions.

The best way to learn any language
is to live with someone who can
only speak that language.

The best thing ever said to me while playing football was after I ran past a surprised linebacker: "Wow, I didn't know you were that fast." Know your capabilities, but don't broadcast them.

No hedge is perfect. Hedging your trading is necessary, but sometimes both sides of the hedged position can move against you.

Buy both calls and puts to be
prepared for the unknown and
unknowable risks. Always know
your ratio of longs to shorts.

During fast unexpected moves options with far off strike dates don't move as much as those with closer strike dates. The far off options don't lose as fast, but they don't win as much either.

When buying calls and puts you always know how much you can lose. The risks of selling calls and puts are more complicated and potential losses can be huge and sometimes infinite.

Think counter intuitively – buy calls after a big fall and buy puts after a huge run up.

Buy out of the money options for the most potential profit, but don't get greedy. Successful options trading is about scoring with singles and doubles, it's not about hitting homeruns.

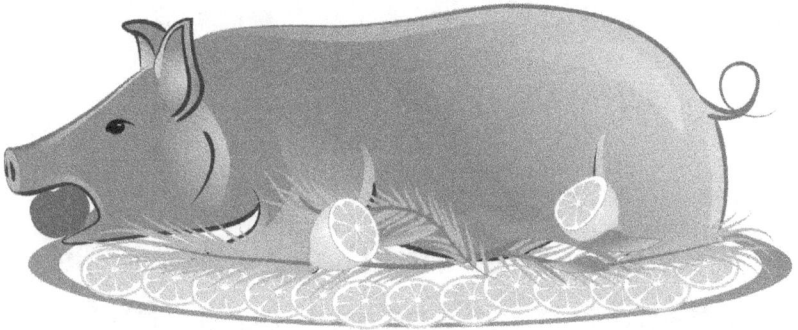

When you enter a losing position, close it out and take your losses. No one gets it right every time; closing out losers is the most important part of trading.

Let your winners run. The least stressful way to do this is to scale your selling over time. When you decide to sell, close out a large enough portion to make yourself comfortable with a slower pace of selling thereafter, say ten or twenty percent at a time.

When the pressure to sell becomes overwhelming in a position you still feel has merit, sell covered calls or buy puts to protect what you have and take the emotion out of the sale.

**Sell calls in flat or bear markets,
sell puts in bull markets.**

**When the situation is confusing,
straddle the position.**

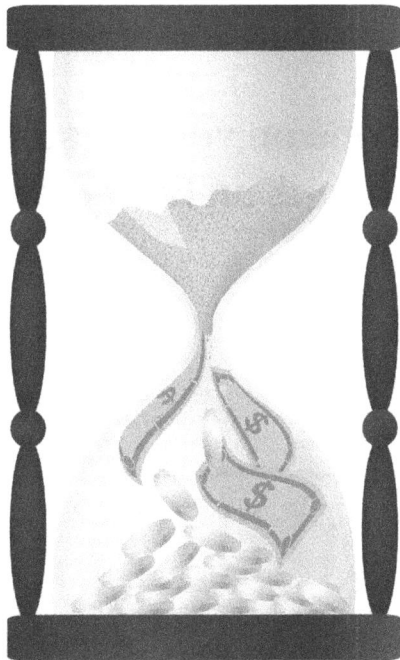

The talking heads on Wall Street need to stay invested; a flea can afford to wait.

Buy options on volatile stocks and sell options on boring stocks.

If a stock moves hard on news, buy options on the reversal. Don't follow the herd. Straddle if you must.

If you take a big loss, resist the temptation to sell into the swoon. Wait for the dead cat bounce.

When trading, listen to a business channel with interviews with Wall Street traders. It doesn't matter what they say, you're listening for the emotions on the street. Floor traders are famous for following the crowd and their emotions telegraph the market trend.

Fears assuaged with Halloween's
passing, but only fools are brave
with April's fasting.

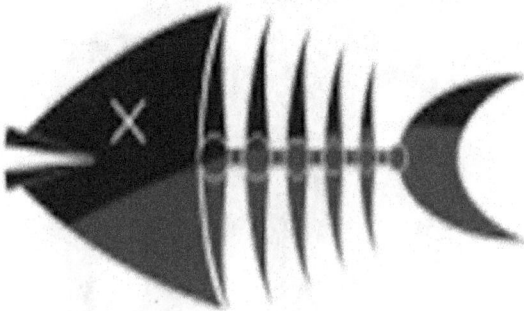

When selecting a stop loss point,
first assume you will hit it. Imagine
the situation and the necessity
to sell for a loss at that moment.
If the loss imagined makes you
uncomfortable, revisit your stop
loss point.

Don't let personal politics control your trades, a liberal can make money in the markets as easily as a conservative.

**Always use limit orders; no reason
to give the sharks a chance to bite.**

No other trade needs a stop loss
plan more than selling naked puts.
No other time is adhering to the
plan more important.

The sooner you sell a loser, the
sooner it stops dominating your
thoughts, regardless of whether it
goes up or down from there.

If is trade is not large enough
to make you sweat, you may be
tempted to let it ride instead of
taking the loss.

The greatest minds in history:
Einstein, Kelvin, Darwin, Pauling,
have made colossal mistakes by
being too sure of their opinions.
The more confident you are, the
more important it is to hedge your
positions.

My dad always said, "When you decide to buy a car, and you are positive about your decision, wait three days then buy it. I've avoided buying dozens of cars by following his advice. Large stock positions are the same.

A public pronouncement tends to cement you into a position.

The most important facet of buying and selling options is your opinion of how the underlying equity will perform over the duration of the contract.

I learned as a bartender that having a drink in front of you does not mean you should drink it. You don't get your money back if you finish your drink (or clean your plate), the money is gone irrespective of your decision to walk away or not. Don't let your decision to buy a position affect your decision to sell it at a loss.

When searching for a new position it is just as important to find stocks you believe will go down as it is to find stocks you believe will go up.

The Endowment Effect—we
humans always think things
are worth more when we own
them. We always want more for
something we are selling than we
would pay for the same thing if we
were buying.

The Status Quo Effect—the human tendency to do nothing. Our preference to maintain a position rather than make a change, bullish or bearish. This is deadly for an options trader, because the clock is always running.

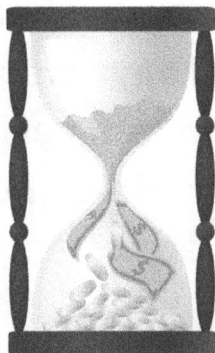

The Disposition Effect – the way excess risk avoidance can cause us to sell our winners too soon and our losers too late.
(This is an ongoing battle for a retired guy with no outside income to compensate for trading mistakes.)

If you want to understand what is happening in the markets you must have money at risk. Fear of losing is the motivation to do the work.

**Holding numerous positions frees
you from falling in love
with any one.**

When it comes to controlling an unruly mustache there is nothing better than a good sneeze.

In 2008 the only safe plays were trading or being out.

During 2013 you didn't need to be a trader, in fact it was a detriment.

In volatile markets the ideal position is one that makes a slow profit under normal circumstances, but will do very little during fast market moves. When the crash is on you can still step out for a cup of coffee and your shorts will cover your longs.

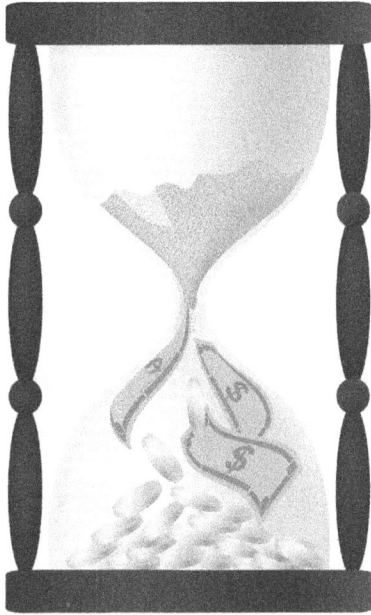

Bubbles are like earthquakes, you know when you are overdue for a disaster, but you never know when the break will come.

You want to get to an emotional
point where you don't feel the pain
of a loss or the ecstasy of a big
win. It's just a job, just numbers –
not money.

Winners tend to burn a hole in your pocket, losers hide behind every piece of lint.

Patience. How soon you get into a position is not as important as recognizing the inflection point, the turn leading to the real move that will last. Technical traders use the **MACD** – moving average convergence divergence.

When selling puts with the intent to
buy stock, stop loss
discipline is paramount.

Books by

JAMES J HOUTS

Spirit of Error

Carnival of Cannibals

Reminiscences of a Stock Market Flea™

The Stock Market Flea™: Trading the Crash of 2008

www.ingramcontent.com/pod-product-compliance
Lightning Source LLC
Chambersburg PA
CBHW060510030426
42337CB00015B/1833